50+*Easy* Classical *Solos* for Violin

Exclusive distributors:
Hal Leonard
7777 West Bluemound Road,
Milwaukee, WI 53213
Email: info@halleonard.com

Hal Leonard Europe Limited
42 Wigmore Street Marylebone,
London, WIU 2 RY
Email: info@halleonardeurope.com

Hal Leonard Australia Pty. Ltd.
4 Lentara Court Cheltenham,
Victoria, 9132 Australia
Email: info@halleonard.com.au

Order No. AM932096
ISBN 0-7119-5191-8
This book © Copyright 1995 by
Hal Leonard

Cover design by Pearce Marchbank,
Studio Twenty
Quarked by Ben May

Printed in EU.

www.halleonard.com

1st Movement Themes
from Symphony No.6 (Pastoral)

Not too fast

Ludwig van Beethoven

1st Movement Theme

Eine Kleine Nachtmusik

K. 525

Bright

Wolfgang Amadeus Mozart

2nd Movement Theme
from Piano Sonata (Pathétique) Op.13

Moderately

Ludwig van Beethoven

2nd Movement Theme
from Symphony No.7

Moderately

Ludwig van Beethoven

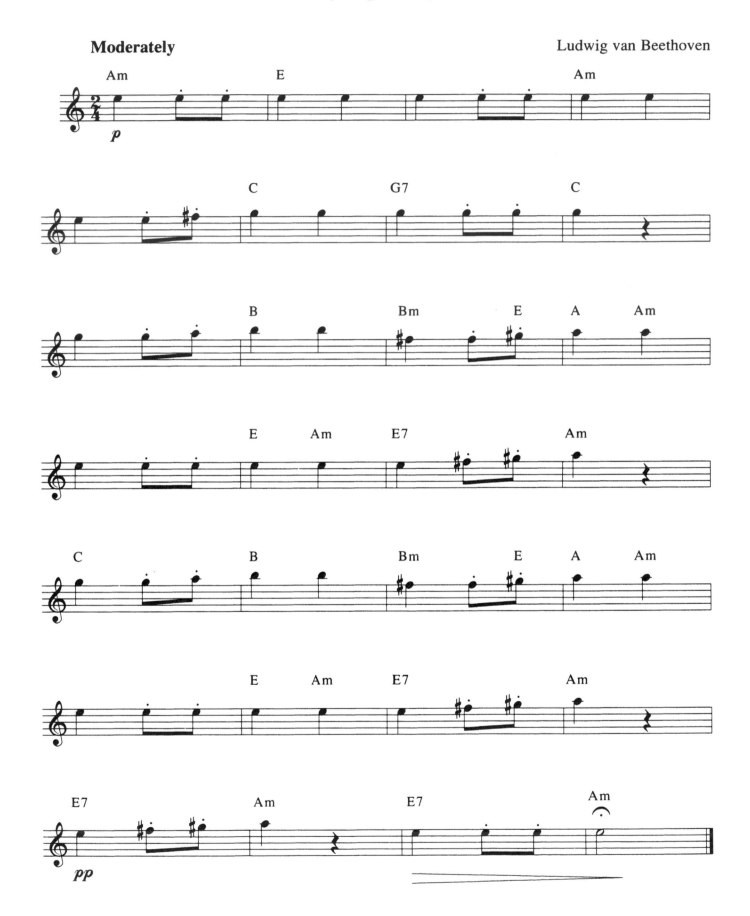

3rd Movement Theme
from Piano Concerto No.1 in C (Rondo) Op.15

Gaily

Ludwig van Beethoven

Air
from The Peasant Cantata

Moderately

Johann Sebastian Bach

Air in D Major
from Orchestral Suite in D

Slow

Johann Sebastian Bach

Ave Verum Corpus

Slow

Wolfgang Amadeus Mozart

Badinerie
from Orchestral Suite in B minor

Bright

Johann Sebastian Bach

Bourrée

Johann Sebastian Bach

Bourrée No. 1
from Orchestral Suite in C

Bright

Johann Sebastian Bach

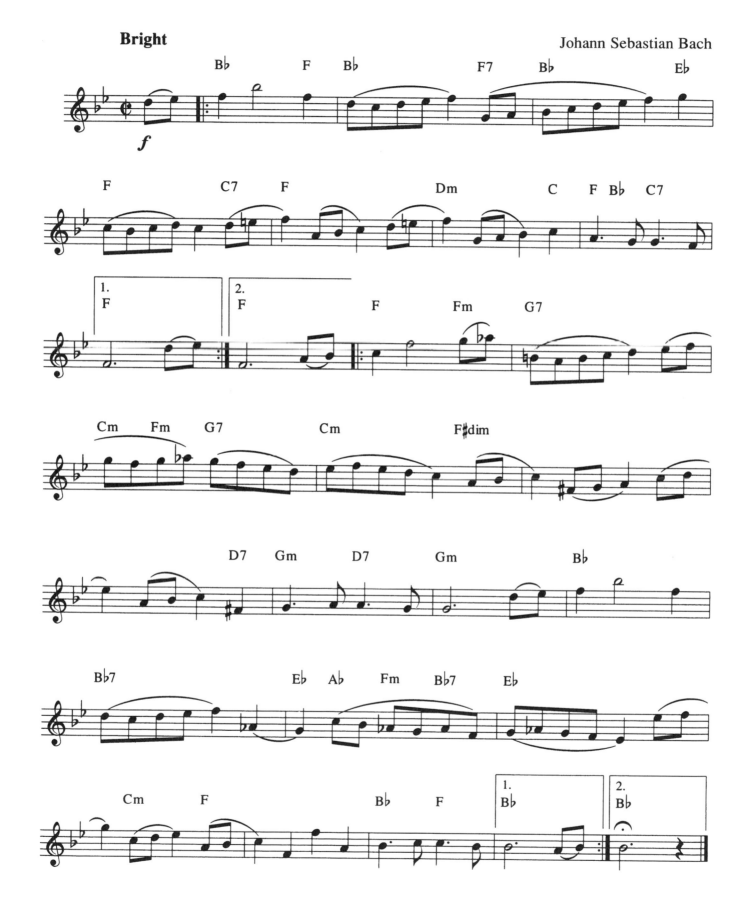

But Who May Abide
from Messiah

Moderately slow

George Frideric Handel

Dead March from Saul

Slow

George Frideric Handel

Elvira Madigan
Theme from Piano Concerto in C Major
K. 467

Wolfgang Amadeus Mozart

Slow

German Dance

Bright

Ludwig van Beethoven

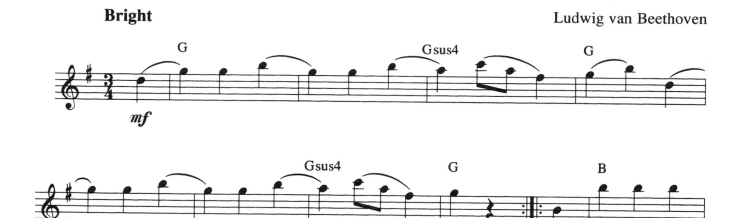

Grand March from Aida

With breadth

Giuseppe Verdi

He Shall Feed His Flock
from Messiah

Moderately

George Frideric Handel

Hornpipe
from Water Music

Bright

George Frideric Handel

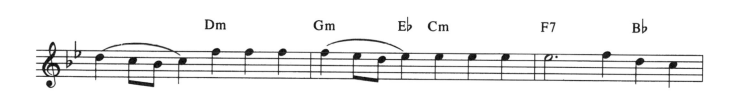

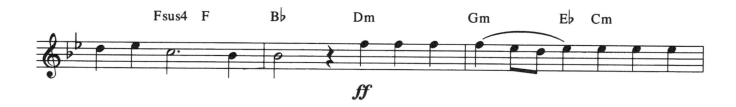

I Know That My Redeemer Liveth
from Messiah

George Frideric Handel

Not too slow

In Tears Of Grief
from St Matthew Passion

Moderately

Johann Sebastian Bach

Jesu, Joy Of Man's Desiring

With easy movement

Johann Sebastian Bach

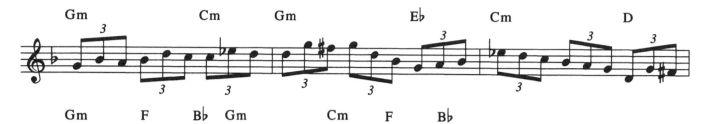

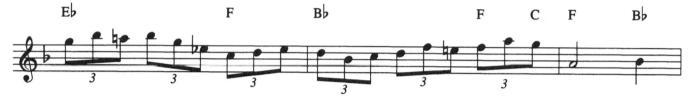

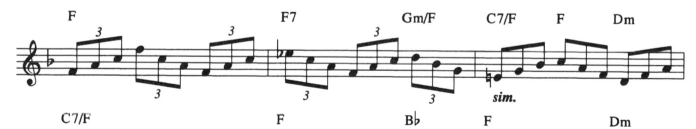

Largo
from Xerxes

George Frideric Handel

Last Movement Theme
from Symphony No. 9 (Ode To Joy)

With movement

Ludwig van Beethoven

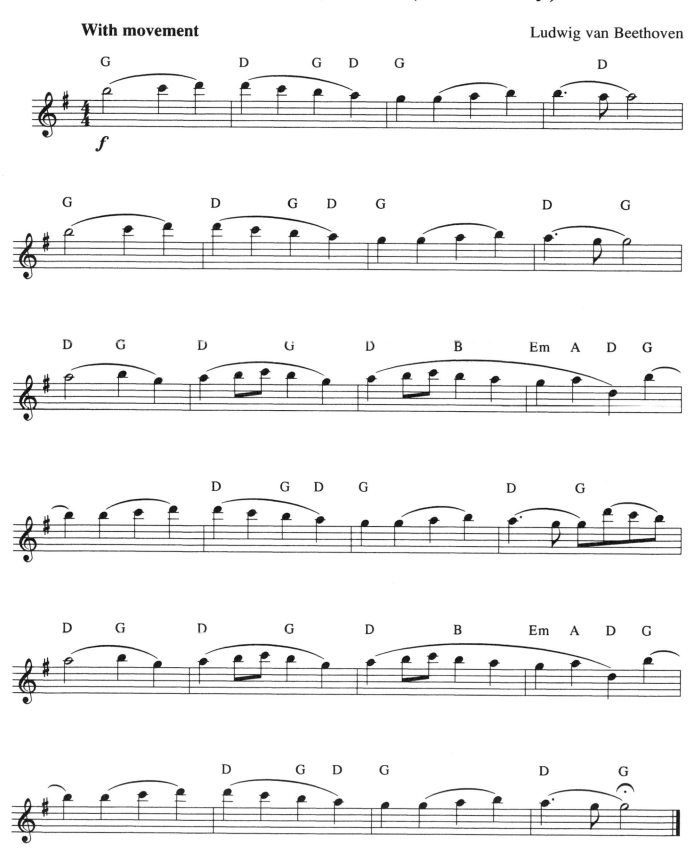

Let The Bright Seraphim
from Samson

With movement

George Frideric Handel

March
from Scipione

With movement

George Frideric Handel

Military March

Bright

Franz Schubert

Minuet in G

Minuet In G

Moderately

Ludwig van Beethoven

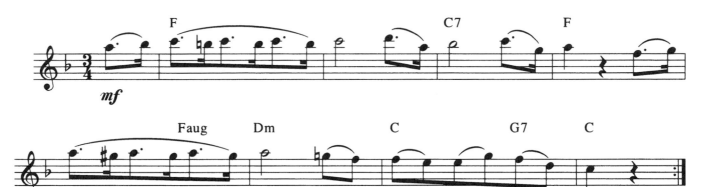

Pomp And Circumstance March No. 1

With grandeur

Sir Edward Elgar

Romance
from Eine Kleine Nachtmusik
K. 525

Slowly

Wolfgang Amadeus Mozart

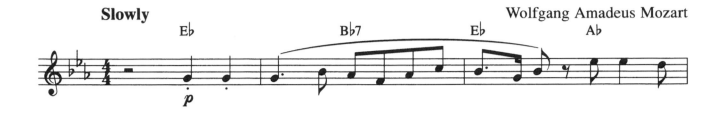

Radetzky March

Bright

Johann Strauss

Rondo Alla Turca
from Sonata in A
K. 300

With movement

Wolfgang Amadeus Mozart

Say Goodbye Now To Pastime
from The Marriage Of Figaro

Bright

Wolfgang Amadeus Mozart

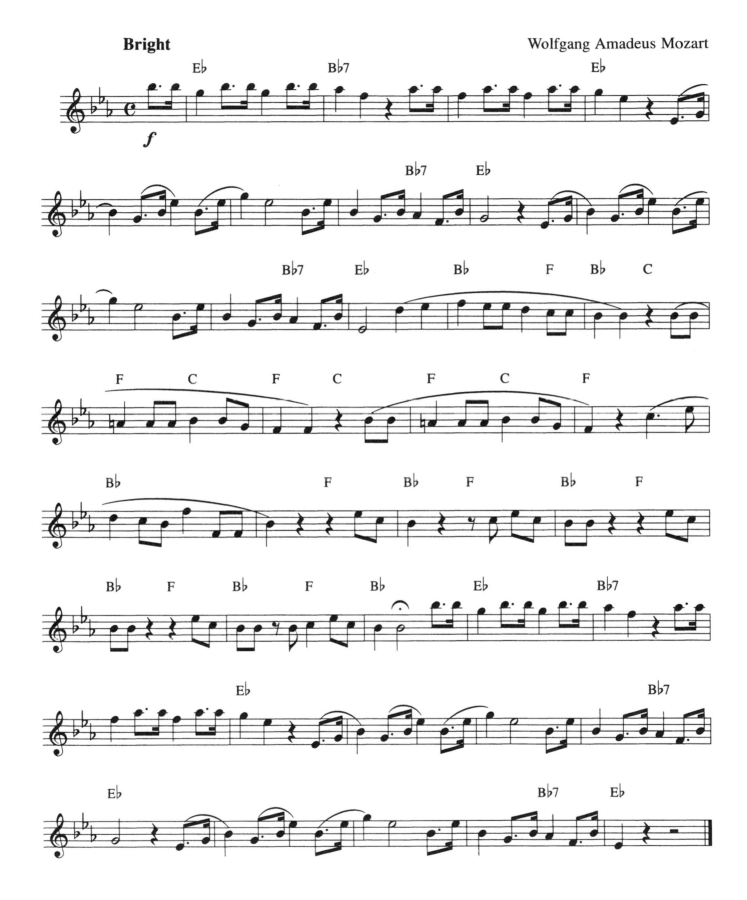

See The Conquering Hero Comes

from Judas Maccabaeus

Majestically

George Frideric Handel

Sheep May Safely Graze

Moderately

Johann Sebastian Bach

Slow Movement Theme
from Symphony No.5

Moderately

Ludwig van Beethoven

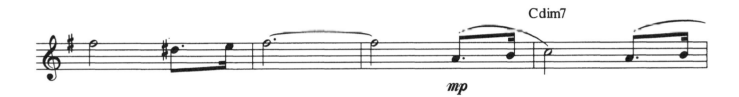

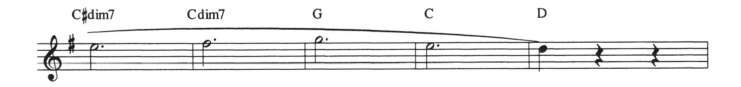

Sleepers, Wake! A Voice Is Calling

Moderately

Johann Sebastian Bach

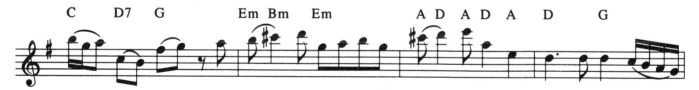

rall.

Sonata in A
1st Movement Theme
K. 300

Moderately

Wolfgang Amadeus Mozart

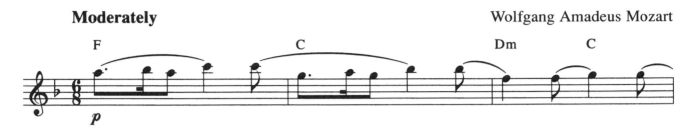

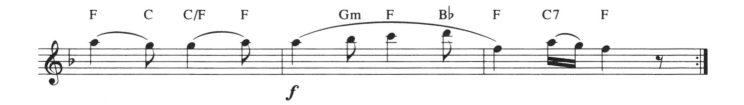

Sonata in C
2nd Movement Theme
K. 545

Slowly

Wolfgang Amadeus Mozart

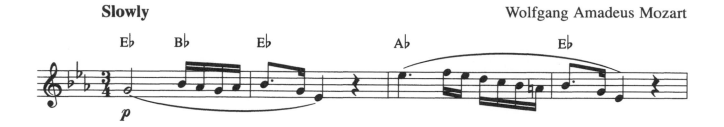

Sonata in C Minor
Last Movement Theme
K. 456

Wolfgang Amadeus Mozart

Bright

Song: "Lullaby"

Moderately

Wolfgang Amadeus Mozart

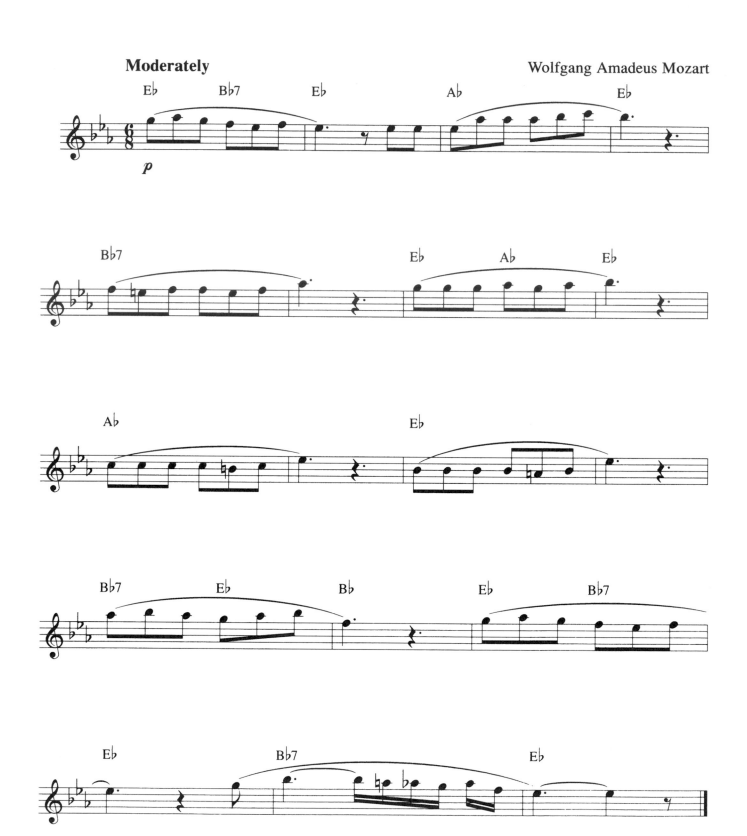

Symphony No.1 in C Minor
4th Movement Theme

Moderately

Johannes Brahms

Symphony No.3 in F
3rd Movement Theme

Johannes Brahms

Symphony No.5
Extract from Andante Cantabile

Slowly and with feeling

Peter Ilyich Tchaikovsky

Symphony No.6 (Pathétique)
1st Movement Theme

Peter Ilyich Tchaikovsky

Symphony No.9 in E Minor
(From The New World)
2nd Movement Theme

Slowly

Antonin Dvořák

Symphony No.9 in E Minor
(From The New World)
Finale

With vigour

Antonin Dvořák

Symphony No.94 in G (Surprise)
2nd Movement Theme

Moderately

Franz Joseph Haydn

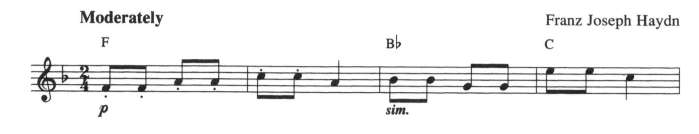

Tell Me Fair Ladies
from The Marriage Of Figaro

Moderately

Wolfgang Amadeus Mozart

Tempo di Menuetto
from Sonata in G, Op. 49, No. 2

Moderately

Ludwig van Beethoven

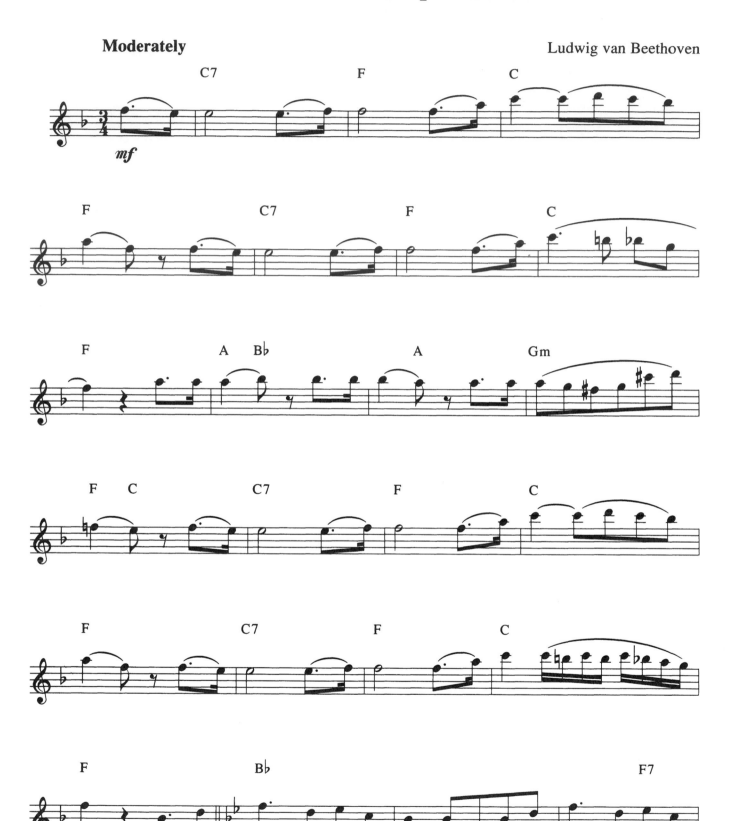

The Manly Heart That Claims Our Duty

from The Magic Flute

Moderately

Wolfgang Amadeus Mozart

Theme from Symphony in G Minor

K. 550

With movement

Wolfgang Amadeus Mozart